Diabetic *Desserts*

Publications International, Ltd.

Nutritional Analysis: Every effort has been made to check the accuracy of the nutritional information that appears with each recipe. However, because numerous variables account for a wide range of values for certain foods, nutritive analyses in this book should be considered approximate. Different results may be obtained by using different nutrient databases and different brand-name products.

Microwave Cooking: Microwave ovens vary in wattage. Use the cooking times as guidelines and check for doneness before adding more time.

Preparation/Cooking Times: Preparation times are based on the approximate amount of time required to assemble the recipe before cooking, baking, chilling or serving. These times include preparation steps such as measuring, chopping and mixing. The fact that some preparations and cooking can be done simultaneously is taken into account. Preparation of optional ingredients and serving suggestions is not included.

Note: This book is for informational purposes and is not intended to provide medical advice. Neither Publications International, Ltd., nor the authors, editors or publisher takes responsibility for any possible consequences from any treatment, procedure, exercise, dietary modification, action, or applications of medication or preparation by any person reading or following the information in this cookbook. The publication of this book does not constitute the practice of medicine, and this cookbook does not replace your physician, pharmacist or health-care specialist. **Before undertaking any course of treatment or nutritional plan, the authors, editors and publisher advise the reader to check with a physician or other health-care provider.**

Not all recipes in this cookbook are appropriate for all people with diabetes. Health-care providers, registered dietitians and certified diabetes educators can help design specific meal plans tailored to individual needs.

Diabetic *Desserts*

chocolate bliss

Creamy Rich Fudge

1½ cups EQUAL® Sugar Lite™
⅔ cup evaporated 2% milk
2 tablespoons butter
¼ teaspoon salt
2 cups miniature marshmallows
1½ cups semisweet chocolate chips
1 teaspoon vanilla extract

Combine EQUAL® Sugar Lite™, evaporated milk, butter and salt in medium-sized heavy saucepan. Bring to a rolling boil over medium heat, stirring frequently. Boil and stir 5 minutes. Remove from heat. Line an 8×8×2-inch pan with foil, with 1 inch hanging over edges.

Mix marshmallows, chocolate chips and vanilla with warm milk mixture; stir until completely melted and smooth. Pour mixture into prepared pan. Chill at least 2 hours or until firm to the touch. Lift fudge out of pan with foil; remove foil and cut into squares. Chill fudge until ready to serve. Keeps tightly covered in refrigerator up to 1 week.

Makes 48 pieces

Nutrients per Serving (2 pieces fudge):
Calories: 106, **Calories from Fat:** 34%, **Total Fat:** 4g,
Saturated Fat: 3g, **Cholesterol:** 3mg, **Sodium:** 37mg,
Carbohydrate: 18g, **Dietary Fiber:** 1g, **Protein:** 1g

Dietary Exchanges: 1 Starch, ½ Fat

Caffè en Forchetta

2 cups reduced-fat (2%) milk
1 cup cholesterol-free egg substitute
½ cup sugar
2 tablespoons no-sugar-added mocha-flavored instant coffee
Grated orange peel or chocolate-covered coffee beans (optional)

1. Preheat oven to 325°F.

2. Combine milk, egg substitute, sugar and instant coffee in medium bowl. Whisk until instant coffee has dissolved and mixture is foamy. Pour into 6 individual custard cups. Place cups in 13×9-inch baking pan. Fill pan with hot water halfway up sides of cups.

3. Bake 55 to 60 minutes or until knife inserted halfway between center and edge comes out clean. Serve warm or at room temperature. Garnish with grated orange peel or chocolate-covered coffee beans, if desired.

Makes 6 servings

Note: Enjoy your after-dinner coffee a whole new way. Translated from Italian, Caffè en Forchetta literally means "coffee on a fork." However, a spoon is recommended for serving this creamy dessert.

Nutrients per Serving (1 cup):
Calories: 111, **Calories from Fat:** 16%, **Total Fat:** 2g, **Saturated Fat:** 1g, **Cholesterol:** 6mg, **Sodium:** 136mg, **Carbohydrate:** 17g, **Dietary Fiber:** 0g, **Protein:** 7g

Dietary Exchanges: 1 Starch, 1 Lean Meat

Rich Chocolate Cheesecake

1 cup chocolate wafer crumbs
3 tablespoons EQUAL® SPOONFUL*
3 tablespoons stick butter or margarine, melted
3 packages (8 ounces each) reduced-fat cream cheese, softened
1¼ cups EQUAL® SPOONFUL**
2 eggs
2 egg whites
2 tablespoons cornstarch
¼ teaspoon salt
1 cup reduced-fat sour cream
2 teaspoons vanilla
4 ounces (4 squares) semi-sweet chocolate, melted and slightly cooled

May substitute 4½ packets EQUAL® sweetener.

**May substitute 30 packets EQUAL® sweetener.*

• Mix chocolate crumbs, 3 tablespoons Equal® Spoonful and melted butter in bottom of 9-inch springform pan. Pat mixture evenly onto bottom of pan. Bake in preheated 325°F oven 8 minutes. Cool on wire rack.

• Beat cream cheese and 1¼ cups Equal® Spoonful in large bowl until fluffy; beat in eggs, egg whites, cornstarch and salt. Beat in sour cream and vanilla until well blended. Gently fold in melted chocolate. Pour batter into crust.

• Bake in 325°F oven 40 to 45 minutes or until center is almost set. Remove cheesecake to wire rack. Gently run metal spatula around rim of pan to loosen cake. Let cheesecake cool completely; cover and refrigerate several hours or overnight before serving. To serve, remove side of springform pan. *Makes 16 servings*

Nutrients per Serving (1 piece cheesecake):
Calories: 219, **Calories from Fat:** 58%, **Total Fat:** 14g, **Saturated Fat:** 9g, **Cholesterol:** 57mg, **Sodium:** 313mg, **Carbohydrate:** 15g, **Dietary Fiber:** 1g, **Protein:** 7g

Dietary Exchanges: 1 Starch, 3 Fat

Chocolate Chip Muffins

1¾ **cups all-purpose flour**
⅓ **cup packed brown sugar**
2 **tablespoons unsweetened cocoa powder**
2½ **teaspoons baking powder**
1½ **teaspoons ground cinnamon**
¼ **teaspoon salt**
1 **cup fat-free (skim) milk**
1 **egg, lightly beaten**
¼ **cup unsweetened applesauce**
2 **tablespoons butter, melted**
1 **teaspoon vanilla**
⅔ **cup miniature semisweet chocolate chips**

1. Preheat oven to 400°F. Spray 12 standard (2½-inch) muffin cups with nonstick cooking spray or line with paper baking cups.

2. Combine flour, brown sugar, cocoa, baking powder, cinnamon and salt in medium bowl. Stir together milk, egg, applesauce, butter and vanilla in small bowl until blended. Add milk mixture to flour mixture; stir just until blended. Fold in chocolate chips.

3. Spoon batter evenly into prepared muffin cups. Bake 13 to 15 minutes or until toothpick inserted into centers comes out clean. Cool in pan on wire rack 5 minutes; remove muffins from pan to wire rack. Serve warm or at room temperature. *Makes 12 servings*

Prep Time: 12 minutes
Bake Time: 13 to 15 minutes

Nutrients per Serving (1 muffin):
Calories: 172, **Calories from Fat:** 28%, **Total Fat:** 6g,
Saturated Fat: 3g, **Cholesterol:** 23mg, **Sodium:** 182mg,
Carbohydrate: 29g, **Dietary Fiber:** 2g, **Protein:** 4g

Dietary Exchanges: 1½ Starch, 1 Fat

Chocolate Fudge Cheesecake Parfaits

1½ **cups fat-free cottage cheese**
   4 **packets sugar substitute** *or* **equivalent of**
      8 **teaspoons sugar**
   2 **teaspoons packed brown sugar**
1½ **teaspoons vanilla**
   2 **tablespoons semisweet mini chocolate chips,**
      divided
   2 **cups fat-free chocolate ice cream or frozen yogurt**
   3 **tablespoons graham cracker crumbs, divided**

1. Combine cottage cheese, sugar substitute, brown sugar and vanilla in food processor or blender; process until smooth. Stir in 1 tablespoon mini chips.

2. Spoon about ¼ cup ice cream into each of 4 stemmed glasses. Top with heaping tablespoon cheese mixture; sprinkle with 2 teaspoons graham cracker crumbs. Repeat layers of ice cream and cheese mixture. Freeze parfaits 15 to 30 minutes to firm slightly.

3. Garnish each parfait with remaining 1 tablespoon mini chips and remaining cracker crumbs.   *Makes 4 servings*

Nutrients per Serving:
Calories: 199, **Calories from Fat:** 9%, **Total Fat:** 2g,
Saturated Fat: 1g, **Cholesterol:** 0mg, **Sodium:** 419mg,
Carbohydrate: 28g, **Dietary Fiber:** 1g, **Protein:** 17g

Dietary Exchanges: 1½ Starch, 1½ Lean Meat

Chocolate-Coffee Napoleons

1 tablespoon instant coffee granules
¼ cup warm water
1 package (4-serving size) chocolate fat-free
    sugar-free instant pudding and pie filling mix
1¾ cups plus 1 teaspoon milk, divided
1 sheet frozen puff pastry dough, thawed
3 tablespoons powdered sugar
2 tablespoons semisweet chocolate chips

1. Preheat oven to 400°F. Dissolve coffee in water in small bowl. Combine pudding mix, 1¾ cups milk and coffee in medium bowl; whisk 2 minutes or until mixture thickens. Cover and refrigerate.

2. Line large baking sheet with parchment paper. Unfold pastry sheet; cut into 3 strips along fold marks. Cut each strip crosswise into thirds. Place on prepared baking sheet. Bake 12 to 15 minutes or until golden brown. Remove to wire rack to cool completely.

3. Blend powdered sugar and remaining 1 teaspoon milk in small bowl until smooth. Cut each pastry square in half crosswise to form 18 pieces. Spread powdered sugar icing over tops of 6 pastry pieces.

4. Place chocolate chips in small resealable food storage bag. Microwave on MEDIUM (50%) 30 seconds or until melted. Cut small piece off one corner of bag; drizzle over iced pastry pieces. Place in refrigerator.

5. Spoon 2 tablespoons pudding over each of 6 pastry pieces. Repeat layers. Top with iced pastry pieces.

Makes 6 napoleons

Nutrients per Serving:
Calories: 148, **Calories from Fat:** 40%, **Total Fat:** 7g,
Saturated Fat: 3g, **Cholesterol:** 8mg, **Sodium:** 252mg,
Carbohydrate: 18g, **Dietary Fiber:** <1g, **Protein:** 4g

Dietary Exchanges: 1 Starch, 1½ Fat

Raspberry-Glazed Brownies with Cheesecake Topping

¾ cup all-purpose flour
9 tablespoons sucralose-sugar blend, divided
¼ cup unsweetened cocoa powder
¾ teaspoon baking powder
⅛ teaspoon salt
1 jar (2½ ounces) prune purée
¼ cup cold coffee or fat-free (skim) milk
1 egg
2 tablespoons canola oil
¾ teaspoon vanilla, divided
¼ cup seedless raspberry fruit spread
2 ounces reduced-fat cream cheese, softened
4½ teaspoons fat-free (skim) milk

1. Preheat oven to 350°F.

2. Combine flour, 7 tablespoons sucralose-sugar blend, cocoa, baking powder and salt in large bowl; stir until blended. Combine prune purée, coffee, egg, oil and ½ teaspoon vanilla in medium bowl; stir until blended. Make well in center of flour mixture; add purée mixture. Stir until blended. Spread batter evenly into ungreased 8-inch square nonstick baking pan.

3. Bake 8 minutes. (Brownies will appear underbaked.) Cool in pan on wire rack.

4. Meanwhile, place raspberry spread in small microwavable bowl. Microwave on HIGH 10 seconds; stir until smooth. Brush evenly over brownies. Beat cream cheese, 4½ teaspoons milk, remaining 2 tablespoons sucralose-sugar blend and ¼ teaspoon vanilla in medium bowl at medium speed of electric mixer until well blended and smooth.

5. To serve, cut brownies into 12 rectangles; top with 1 teaspoon cream cheese mixture. *Makes 12 servings*

Nutrients per Serving:
Calories: 143, **Calories from Fat:** 24%, **Total Fat:** 4g, **Saturated Fat:** 1g, **Cholesterol:** 20mg, **Sodium:** 85mg, **Carbohydrate:** 24g, **Dietary Fiber:** 1g, **Protein:** 2g

Dietary Exchanges: 1½ Starch, 1 Fat

Chocolate Cream Dessert Dip

  1 package (4-serving size) chocolate fat-free
      sugar-free instant pudding and pie filling mix
  2 cups fat-free (skim) milk
  1 container (8 ounces) fat-free nondairy whipped
      topping
  2 tablespoons mini chocolate chips

Whisk pudding mix and milk in medium bowl 2 minutes. Stir in whipped topping and chocolate pieces. Refrigerate until ready to serve. *Makes 24 servings*

Nutrients per Serving (2 tablespoons):
Calories: 33, **Calories from Fat:** 9%, **Total Fat:** <1g,
Saturated Fat: <1g, **Cholesterol:** <1mg, **Sodium:** 38mg,
Carbohydrate: 6g, **Dietary Fiber:** 0g, **Protein:** <1g

Dietary Exchanges: ½ Starch

Frozen Fudge Pops

  ½ cup fat-free sweetened condensed milk
  ¼ cup unsweetened cocoa powder
  1¼ cups evaporated skimmed milk
  1 teaspoon vanilla

1. Beat sweetened condensed milk and cocoa in medium bowl. Add evaporated milk and vanilla; beat until smooth.

2. Pour mixture into 8 small paper cups or 8 popsicle molds. Freeze about 2 hours or until almost firm. Insert wooden popsicle stick into center of each cup; freeze until solid.
Makes 8 pops

Nutrients per Serving (1 frozen pop):
Calories: 92, **Calories from Fat:** 1%, **Total Fat:** <1g,
Saturated Fat: <1g, **Cholesterol:** 2mg, **Sodium:** 70mg,
Carbohydrate: 17g, **Dietary Fiber:** 0g, **Protein:** 5g

Dietary Exchanges: 1 Milk

Refreshing Cocoa-Fruit Sherbet

> 1 ripe medium banana
> 1½ cups orange juice
> 1 cup (½ pint) half-and-half
> ½ cup sugar
> ¼ cup HERSHEY'S Cocoa

1. Slice banana into blender container. Add orange juice; cover and blend until smooth. Add remaining ingredients; cover and blend well. Pour into 8- or 9-inch square pan. Cover; freeze until hard around edges.

2. Spoon partially frozen mixture into blender container or large bowl. Cover; blend until smooth but not melted. Pour into 1-quart mold. Cover; freeze until firm. Unmold onto cold plate and slice. *Makes 8 servings*

Variation: Add 2 teaspoons orange-flavored liqueur with orange juice.

Nutrients per Serving:
Calories: 130, **Calories from Fat:** 26%, **Total Fat:** 4g, **Saturated Fat:** 2g, **Cholesterol:** 11mg, **Sodium:** 13mg, **Carbohydrate:** 23g, **Dietary Fiber:** 1g, **Protein:** 2g

Dietary Exchanges: 1½ Starch, ½ Fat

Chocolate Mousse

½ **cup plus 2 tablespoons sugar, divided**
¼ **cup unsweetened cocoa powder**
 1 **envelope unflavored gelatin**
 2 **tablespoons coffee-flavored liqueur**
 2 **cups fat-free (skim) milk**
¼ **cup cholesterol-free egg substitute**
 2 **egg whites**
⅛ **teaspoon cream of tartar**
½ **cup reduced-fat nondairy whipped topping**

1. Combine ½ cup sugar, cocoa and gelatin in medium saucepan. Add liqueur; let stand 2 minutes. Add milk; heat over medium heat. Stir until sugar and gelatin are dissolved. Stir in egg substitute. Set aside.

2. Beat egg whites in medium bowl with electric mixer until foamy; add cream of tartar. Beat until soft peaks form Gradually beat in remaining 2 tablespoons sugar; continue beating until stiff peaks form.

3. Gently fold egg whites into cocoa mixture. Fold in whipped topping. Divide evenly between 8 dessert dishes. Refrigerate until thickened.   *Makes 8 servings*

Nutrients per Serving:
Calories: 125, **Calories from Fat:** 6%, **Total Fat:** 1g,
Saturated Fat: 1g, **Cholesterol:** 1mg, **Sodium:** 60mg,
Carbohydrate: 23g, **Dietary Fiber:** <1g, **Protein:** 5g

Dietary Exchanges: 1½ Starch

fruit
finales

Cinnamon Fruit Crisp

      4 medium unpeeled nectarines (about 1½ pounds)
      2 large unpeeled plums (about 8 ounces)
      5 tablespoons sugar substitute,* divided
  1½ teaspoons ground cinnamon, divided
    ¼ cup all-purpose flour
    ¼ cup uncooked old-fashioned oats
      3 tablespoons cold butter, cut into pieces
    ¼ cup pecan chips, toasted

This recipe was tested with sucralose-based sugar substitute.

1. Preheat oven to 375°F.

2. Cut nectarines and plums into slices over medium bowl to catch any juices; discard pits. Combine 2 tablespoons sugar substitute and 1 teaspoon cinnamon in small bowl; sprinkle over fruit. Mix well. Transfer fruit mixture to 9-inch pie plate.

3. Combine flour, oats, remaining 3 tablespoons sugar substitute and remaining ½ teaspoon cinnamon in small bowl. Cut in butter with pastry blender or two knives until mixture resembles coarse crumbs. Stir in pecans; sprinkle oat mixture over fruit mixture.

4. Bake 30 minutes or until filling is bubbly and topping is golden brown. Serve warm or at room temperature.

Makes 6 servings

Nutrients per Serving (½ cup crisp):
Calories: 177, **Calories from Fat:** 51%, **Total Fat:** 10g,
Saturated Fat: 4g, **Cholesterol:** 15mg, **Sodium:** 41mg,
Carbohydrate: 24g, **Dietary Fiber:** 3g, **Protein:** 3g

Dietary Exchanges: ½ Starch, 1 Fruit, 2 Fat

Dessert Nachos

3 (6- to 7-inch) flour tortillas
Nonstick cooking spray
1 tablespoon sugar
⅛ teaspoon ground cinnamon
Dash ground allspice
1 container (6 ounces) vanilla sugar-free fat-free
   yogurt
1 teaspoon grated orange peel
1½ cups strawberries
½ cup blueberries
4 teaspoons miniature semisweet chocolate chips

1. Preheat oven to 375°F.

2. Cut each tortilla into 8 wedges. Place on ungreased baking sheet. Generously spray tortilla wedges with cooking spray. Combine sugar, cinnamon and allspice in small bowl. Sprinkle over tortilla wedges. Bake 7 to 9 minutes or until lightly browned; cool completely.

3. Meanwhile, combine yogurt and orange peel. Stem strawberries; cut lengthwise into quarters.

4. Place 6 tortilla wedges on each of 4 small plates. Top with strawberries and blueberries. Drizzle with yogurt mixture. Sprinkle with chocolate chips. Serve immediately.

Makes 4 servings

Nutrients per Serving:
Calories: 160, **Calories from Fat:** 19%, **Total Fat:** 3g,
Saturated Fat: 1g, **Cholesterol:** 2mg, **Sodium:** 146mg,
Carbohydrate: 28g, **Dietary Fiber:** 3g, **Protein:** 4g

Dietary Exchanges: 1 Starch, 1 Fruit, ½ Fat

Blackberry Strudel Cups

6 sheets frozen phyllo dough, thawed
   Nonstick cooking spray
1 pint blackberries
2 tablespoons sugar
1 cup reduced-fat nondairy whipped topping
1 container (6 ounces) apricot low-fat custard-style
   yogurt

1. Preheat oven to 400°F. Unroll phyllo dough keeping sheets in stack. Cover with plastic wrap and damp kitchen towel. Place 1 sheet of phyllo dough on work surface. Cut crosswise into 4 pieces. Lightly coat first piece with cooking spray; place in large custard cup. Place second piece on top of first, alternating corners; spray with cooking spray. Repeat with remaining 2 pieces. Repeat with remaining sheets of phyllo dough to form 5 more strudel cups. Place custard cups on baking sheet. Bake about 15 minutes or until pastry is golden. Let cool to room temperature.

2. Meanwhile, combine blackberries and sugar in small bowl; let stand 15 minutes. Mix whipped topping and yogurt in medium bowl. Reserve ½ cup blackberries for garnish; gently stir remaining blackberries into whipped topping mixture. Spoon into cooled pastry cups. Top with reserved blackberries. *Makes 6 servings*

Nutrients per Serving (1 strudel cup):
Calories: 125, **Calories from Fat:** 22%, **Total Fat:** 4g,
Saturated Fat: <1g, **Cholesterol:** 3mg, **Sodium:** 22mg,
Carbohydrate: 25g, **Dietary Fiber:** 3g, **Protein:** 3g

Dietary Exchanges: 1½ Fruit, 1 Fat

Pears with Apricot-Ginger Sauce

¼ **cup water**
4 **whole firm pears, peeled with stems attached**
1 **tablespoon lemon juice**
2 **tablespoons apricot fruit spread**
1 **teaspoon grated fresh ginger**
½ **teaspoon vanilla**
½ **teaspoon cornstarch**

SLOW COOKER DIRECTIONS

1. Coat slow cooker with nonstick cooking spray. Add water and arrange pears, stem side up. Spoon lemon juice over pears. Cover; cook on HIGH 2½ hours.

2. Remove pears and set aside on serving platter.

3. Combine fruit spread, ginger, vanilla and cornstarch in small bowl. Stir until cornstarch dissolves.

4. Add mixture to water remaining in slow cooker; whisk until blended. Cover; cook on HIGH 15 minutes or until sauce thickens slightly. Spoon sauce over pears. Serve warm or at room temperature.   *Makes 4 servings*

Nutrients per Serving:
Calories: 120, **Calories from Fat:** 1%, **Total Fat:** <1g,
Saturated Fat: <1g, **Cholesterol:** 0mg, **Sodium:** 2mg,
Carbohydrate: 31g, **Dietary Fiber:** 5g, **Protein:** 1g

Dietary Exchanges: 2 Fruit

Raspberry Napoleons

1¼ cups low-fat (1%) milk
1 package (4-serving size) vanilla or French vanilla
    instant pudding and pie filling mix
1 tablespoon amaretto liqueur *or* ¼ teaspoon almond
    extract
6 sheets frozen phyllo dough, thawed
    Nonstick cooking spray
2 cups fresh raspberries
2 teaspoons powdered sugar

1. Place milk in medium bowl. Add pudding mix; whisk 2 minutes. Stir in amaretto; cover and refrigerate.

2. Preheat oven to 350°F. Unroll phyllo dough keeping sheets in a stack. Cover with plastic wrap and damp kitchen towel. Place 1 sheet of phyllo dough on large work surface; coat lightly with nonstick cooking spray. Top with two more sheets of phyllo dough, spraying each with cooking spray. Cut stacked dough crosswise into 6 strips. Cut each strip in half to form 12 rectangles. Transfer rectangles to ungreased baking sheet. Repeat with remaining 3 sheets of phyllo dough; place on second baking sheet. Bake 6 to 8 minutes or until golden brown and crisp. Remove to wire racks to cool completely.

3. To assemble, spread half of pudding over 8 rectangles; top with half of raspberries. Repeat layers with 8 phyllo rectangles, remaining pudding and raspberries; top with remaining 8 phyllo rectangles. Sprinkle with powdered sugar before serving.   *Makes 8 servings*

Nutrients per Serving:
Calories: 130, **Calories from Fat:** 12%, **Total Fat:** 2g,
Saturated Fat: 1g, **Cholesterol:** 3mg, **Sodium:** 253mg,
Carbohydrate: 25g, **Dietary Fiber:** 2g, **Protein:** 3g

Dietary Exchanges: 1 Starch, ½ Fruit, ½ Fat

Mangoes and Sweet Cream

½ cup low-fat vanilla yogurt
2 ounces reduced-fat cream cheese, softened
1 packet sugar substitute
¼ teaspoon vanilla
1 medium mango, peeled and diced *or* 1 cup diced
   peaches

Beat yogurt, cream cheese, sugar substitute and vanilla in small bowl with electric mixer at medium speed until smooth. Fold in mangoes. Spoon mixture into dessert dishes.

Makes 2 servings

Nutrients per Serving:
Calories: 185, **Calories from Fat:** 26%, **Total Fat:** 5g,
Saturated Fat: 4g, **Cholesterol:** 16mg, **Sodium:** 175mg,
Carbohydrate: 28g, **Dietary Fiber:** 2g, **Protein:** 6g

Dietary Exchanges: 2 Fruit, 1 Fat

Yogurt "Custard" with Blueberries

1 container (6 ounces) plain fat-free yogurt
2 teaspoons honey
⅛ teaspoon ground nutmeg
½ cup fresh or thawed frozen blueberries
1 tablespoon blueberry or raspberry fruit spread
1 tablespoon sliced almonds, toasted

1. Spoon yogurt into paper towel-lined strainer. Place over bowl and refrigerate 20 minutes to drain and thicken.

2. Combine yogurt, honey and nutmeg in small bowl. Combine blueberries and preserves; spoon over yogurt. Top with almonds. *Makes 1 serving*

Nutrients per Serving:
Calories: 273, **Calories from Fat:** 17%, **Total Fat:** 5g,
Saturated Fat: <1g, **Cholesterol:** 3mg, **Sodium:** 135mg,
Carbohydrate: 47g, **Dietary Fiber:** 3g, **Protein:** 12g

Dietary Exchanges: 2½ Fruit, 1 Milk, 1 Fat

Peaches with Raspberry Sauce

1 cup raspberries
½ cup water
¼ cup measure-for-measure sugar substitute
6 peach halves
6 tablespoons vanilla low-fat yogurt

1. Combine raspberries, water and sugar substitute in small saucepan. Bring to a boil. Boil 1 minute. Place in blender or food processor and process until smooth. Set aside. Let cool 15 minutes.

2. Drizzle raspberry sauce on each of 6 serving dishes. Place one peach half on each dish. Spoon 1 tablespoon yogurt over each peach half.   *Makes 6 servings*

Nutrients per Serving (½ peach, ¼ cup sauce and 1 tablespoon yogurt per serving):
Calories: 41, **Calories from Fat:** 8%, **Total Fat:** 0g, **Saturated Fat:** 0g, **Cholesterol:** <1mg, **Sodium:** 9mg, **Carbohydrate:** 10g, **Dietary Fiber:** 2g, **Protein:** 1g

Dietary Exchanges: ½ Fruit

Pineapple-Ginger Bavarians

1 can (8 ounces) crushed pineapple in juice, drained and liquid reserved
1 package (4-serving size) orange sugar-free gelatin
1 cup sugar-free ginger ale
1 cup plain fat-free yogurt
¾ teaspoon grated fresh ginger
½ cup whipping cream
1 packet sugar substitute
¼ teaspoon vanilla

1. Combine reserved pineapple juice with enough water to equal ½ cup liquid. Pour into small saucepan; bring to a boil over high heat.

2. Place gelatin in medium bowl. Add pineapple juice mixture; stir until gelatin is completely dissolved. Add ginger ale and half of crushed pineapple; stir until well blended. Add yogurt; whisk until well blended. Pour into 5 individual ramekins. Cover and refrigerate until firm.

3. Meanwhile, combine remaining half of pineapple and ginger in small bowl. Cover with plastic wrap; refrigerate.

4. Just before serving, beat cream in small deep bowl with electric mixer at high speed until soft peaks form. Add sugar substitute and vanilla; beat until stiff peaks form.

5. Top each Bavarian with 1 tablespoon whipped cream and 1 tablespoon pineapple mixture.   *Makes 5 servings*

Tip: To save time, garnish each serving with 1 tablespoon thawed frozen whipped topping, if desired.

Nutrients per Serving:
Calories: 147, **Calories from Fat:** 56%, **Total Fat:** 9g, **Saturated Fat:** 6g, **Cholesterol:** 34mg, **Sodium:** 111mg, **Carbohydrate:** 12g, **Dietary Fiber:** <1g, **Protein:** 4g

Dietary Exchanges: 1 Starch, 1½ Fat

Strawberry Banana Cream Trifle

        1 pound strawberries, sliced
        ½ cup sugar substitute
        1 package (4-serving size) strawberry sugar-free
            gelatin
        1 cup boiling water
        1 cup ice water
        1 package (4-serving size) banana cream fat-free
            sugar-free instant pudding and pie filling mix
     1¾ cups fat-free (skim) milk
        1 angel food cake (about 10 ounces), cut into thirds
            horizontally

1. Toss strawberries with sugar substitute in medium bowl; set aside.

2. Stir gelatin into boiling water in medium bowl until completely dissolved. Stir in ice water. Freeze 5 minutes until soft-set.

3. Mix pudding and milk in medium bowl with electric mixer at medium speed 2 minutes. Refrigerate 5 minutes to soft-set.

4. Arrange half of angel food cake in bottom of trifle bowl, tearing pieces to fill any gaps.

5. Combine gelatin and pudding until well blended. Stir in strawberries. Spoon half of strawberry mixture over cake.

6. Layer remaining angel food cake on top. Spoon remaining strawberry mixture over cake. Cover and refrigerate 2 hours or until set.   *Makes 20 servings*

Nutrients per Serving (½ cup trifle):
Calories: 59, **Calories from Fat:** 3%, **Total Fat:** 0g,
Saturated Fat: 0g, **Cholesterol:** 0mg, **Sodium:** 186mg,
Carbohydrate: 13g, **Dietary Fiber:** <1g, **Protein:** 2g

Dietary Exchanges: 1 Starch

Peaches & Cream Gingersnap Cups

1½ tablespoons gingersnap crumbs (2 cookies)
¼ teaspoon ground ginger
2 ounces reduced-fat cream cheese, softened
1 container (6 ounces) peach sugar-free fat-free yogurt
¼ teaspoon vanilla
⅓ cup chopped fresh peaches or drained canned peach slices in juice

1. Combine gingersnap crumbs and ginger in small bowl; set aside.

2. Beat cream cheese in medium bowl with electric mixer at medium speed until smooth. Add yogurt and vanilla. Beat at low speed until smooth and well blended. Stir in chopped peaches.

3. Divide peach mixture between two 6-ounce custard cups. Cover and refrigerate 1 hour. Top each serving with half of gingersnap crumb mixture just before serving.

Makes 2 servings

Nutrients per Serving:
Calories: 148, **Calories from Fat:** 34%, **Total Fat:** 5g,
Saturated Fat: 3g, **Cholesterol:** 16mg, **Sodium:** 204mg,
Carbohydrate: 18g, **Dietary Fiber:** 1g, **Protein:** 6g

Dietary Exchanges: 1 Starch, ½ Milk, 1 Fat

oven
treats

Easy Fruit Tarts

12 wonton skins
    Vegetable cooking spray
2 tablespoons apple jelly or apricot fruit spread
1½ cups sliced or cut-up fruit such as DOLE® Bananas,
    Strawberries or Red or Green Seedless Grapes
1 cup nonfat or low-fat yogurt, any flavor

• Press wonton skins into 12 muffin cups sprayed with vegetable cooking spray, allowing corners to stand up over edges of muffin cups.

• Bake at 375°F 5 minutes or until lightly browned. Carefully remove wonton cups to wire rack; cool.

• Cook and stir jelly in small saucepan over low heat until jelly melts.

• Brush bottoms of cooled wonton cups with melted jelly. Place two fruit slices in each cup; spoon rounded tablespoon of yogurt on top of fruit. Garnish with fruit slice and mint leaves. Serve immediately. *Makes 12 servings*

Prep Time: 20 minutes
Bake Time: 5 minutes

Nutrients per Serving (1 tart):
Calories: 57, **Calories from Fat:** 5%, **Total Fat:** <1g,
Saturated Fat: <1g, **Cholesterol:** 2mg, **Sodium:** 32mg,
Carbohydrate: 12g, **Dietary Fiber:** 1g, **Protein:** 1g

Dietary Exchanges: 1 Fruit

Hidden Pumpkin Pies

1½ **cups canned solid-pack pumpkin**
1 **cup evaporated skimmed milk**
½ **cup cholesterol-free egg substitute** *or* 2 **eggs**
¼ **cup sugar substitute***
1¼ **teaspoons vanilla, divided**
1 **teaspoon pumpkin pie spice****
3 **egg whites**
¼ **teaspoon cream of tartar**
⅓ **cup honey**

This recipe was tested with sucralose-based sugar substitute.

**Substitute ½ teaspoon ground cinnamon, ¼ teaspoon ground ginger and ⅛ teaspoon each ground allspice and ground nutmeg for 1 teaspoon pumpkin pie spice, if desired.*

1. Preheat oven to 350°F.

2. Combine pumpkin, evaporated milk, egg substitute, sugar substitute, pumpkin pie spice and 1 teaspoon vanilla in large bowl. Pour into 6 (6-ounce) custard cups or soufflé dishes. Place in shallow baking dish or pan. Pour boiling water around custard cups to depth of 1 inch. Bake 25 minutes or until set.

3. Meanwhile, beat egg whites, cream of tartar and remaining ¼ teaspoon vanilla in medium bowl with electric mixer at high speed until soft peaks form. Gradually add honey, beating until stiff peaks form.

4. Spread egg white mixture over top of hot pumpkin pies. Return to oven. Bake 8 to 12 minutes or until tops of pies are golden brown. Let stand 10 minutes. Serve warm.

Makes 6 servings

Nutrients per Serving (1 pie):
Calories: 148, **Calories from Fat:** 10%, **Total Fat:** 2g,
Saturated Fat: 1g, **Cholesterol:** 54mg, **Sodium:** 133mg,
Carbohydrate: 27g, **Dietary Fiber:** 2g, **Protein:** 8g

Dietary Exchanges: 2 Starch, 1 Lean Meat

Southern Peanut Butter Cheesecake

½ cup low-fat graham cracker crumbs
8 ounces cream cheese, softened and cut into cubes
8 ounces fat-free cream cheese, cut into cubes
½ cup fat-free sour cream
½ cup fat-free ricotta or low-fat cottage cheese
⅓ cup peanut butter
½ cup firmly packed dark brown sugar
2 teaspoons vanilla extract
6 egg whites *or* **¾ cup egg substitute**

Coat a 9-inch springform pan with cooking spray. Sprinkle graham cracker crumbs evenly over the bottom of pan. Set aside. Process the cream cheese, sour cream and ricotta cheese in a food processor until smooth. Add the peanut butter and mix. Slowly add the sugar and vanilla extract. Slowly pour the eggs through the food chute with the processor running. Process until blended. Spoon the mixture over the graham cracker crumbs. Bake in a preheated 300°F oven for 50 minutes. Center will be soft, but will firm when chilled. Turn the oven off and leave the cheesecake in the oven for 30 minutes more. Remove from oven; let cool to room temperature on a wire rack. Cover and chill 8 hours. Garnish with chopped peanuts or serve with assorted fresh berries, if desired. *Makes 10 servings*

Favorite recipe from **Peanut Advisory Board**

Nutrients per Serving (1 slice cheesecake):
Calories: 140, **Calories from Fat:** 29%, **Total Fat:** 5g, **Saturated Fat:** 2g, **Cholesterol:** 10mg, **Sodium:** 240mg, **Carbohydrate:** 14g, **Dietary Fiber:** 0g, **Protein:** 13g

Dietary Exchanges: 1 Starch, 1 Lean Meat, ½ Fat

Peach Pecan Upside-Down Pancake

2 tablespoons butter, melted
2 tablespoons packed light brown sugar
1 tablespoon maple syrup
8 ounces (½ package) frozen unsweetened peach
    slices, thawed
2 to 3 tablespoons pecan pieces
2 eggs
⅓ cup milk
½ teaspoon vanilla
⅔ cup biscuit baking mix
    Additional maple syrup (optional)

1. Preheat oven to 400°F. Spray 8- or 9-inch pie pan with nonstick cooking spray.

2. Pour butter into pie pan. Sprinkle with brown sugar and drizzle with maple syrup. Place peach slices in single layer on top in a circle. Sprinkle with pecans; set aside.

3. Whisk together eggs, milk and vanilla in medium bowl. Stir in baking mix until just combined. Pour batter over peaches.

4. Bake 15 to 18 minutes until lightly browned and firm to the touch. Let cool 1 minute. Run knife around outer edge; invert pancake onto serving plate. Serve immediately with additional maple syrup, if desired.   *Makes 6 servings*

Nutrients per Serving (1 wedge):
Calories: 175, **Calories from Fat:** 47%, **Total Fat:** 9g,
Saturated Fat: 4g, **Cholesterol:** 82mg, **Sodium:** 223mg,
Carbohydrate: 20g, **Dietary Fiber:** <1g, **Protein:** 4g

Dietary Exchanges: 1 Starch, ½ Fruit, 1½ Fat

Cranberry-Orange Bread Pudding

2 cups (4 slices) cubed cinnamon bread
¼ cup dried cranberries
2 cups low-fat (1%) milk
½ cup cholesterol-free egg substitute
1 package (4-serving size) vanilla sugar-free cook and
    serve pudding and pie filling mix*
1 teaspoon grated orange peel
1 teaspoon vanilla
½ teaspoon ground cinnamon

*Do not use instant pudding and pie filling mix.

1. Preheat oven to 325°F. Spray 9 (4-ounce) custard cups with nonstick cooking spray.

2. Evenly divide bread cubes among custard cups; bake 10 minutes. Sprinkle evenly with cranberries.

3. Combine milk, egg substitute, pudding mix, orange peel, vanilla and cinnamon in medium bowl. Carefully pour into custard cups. Let stand 5 to 10 minutes.

4. Place cups on baking sheet. Bake 25 to 30 minutes or until centers are almost set. Let stand 10 minutes. Serve with ice cream, if desired.   *Makes 9 servings*

Nutrients per Serving:
Calories: 67, **Calories from Fat:** 13%, **Total Fat:** 1g,
Saturated Fat: <1g, **Cholesterol:** 2mg, **Sodium:** 190mg,
Carbohydrate: 11g, **Dietary Fiber:** <1g, **Protein:** 4g

Dietary Exchanges: 1 Starch

Boston Babies

1 package (18¼ ounces) yellow cake mix
3 eggs *or* ¾ cup cholesterol-free egg substitute
⅓ cup unsweetened applesauce
1 package (4-serving size) vanilla fat-free sugar-free
    instant pudding and pie filling mix
2 cups low-fat (1%) milk or fat-free (skim) milk
⅓ cup sugar
⅓ cup unsweetened cocoa powder
1 tablespoon cornstarch
1½ cups water
1½ teaspoons vanilla

1. Line 24 standard (2½-inch) muffin cups with paper baking cups.

2. Prepare cake mix according to lower fat package directions, using 3 eggs and applesauce. Spoon batter into prepared muffin cups. Bake according to package directions; cool completely. Freeze 12 cupcakes for another use.

3. Prepare pudding mix according to package directions, using 2 cups milk; cover and refrigerate.

4. For chocolate glaze, combine sugar, cocoa, cornstarch and water in large microwavable bowl; whisk until smooth. Microwave on HIGH 4 to 6 minutes, stirring every 2 minutes, until slightly thickened. Stir in vanilla.

5. For each serving, drizzle 2 tablespoons chocolate glaze onto plate. Top with 2 cupcake halves and 2 heaping tablespoonfuls pudding.   *Makes 12 servings*

Nutrients per Serving:
Calories: 158, **Calories from Fat:** 22%, **Total Fat:** 4g,
Saturated Fat: 1g, **Cholesterol:** 29mg, **Sodium:** 175mg,
Carbohydrate: 28g, **Dietary Fiber:** <1g, **Protein:** 3g

Dietary Exchanges: 2 Starch, ½ Fat

Lemon Pound Cake with Strawberries

2 cups all-purpose flour
1 teaspoon baking powder
1 teaspoon baking soda
½ teaspoon salt
½ cup reduced-fat sour cream
½ cup fat-free (skim) milk
⅓ cup sugar
¼ cup vegetable oil
¼ cup cholesterol-free egg substitute
1 teaspoon grated lemon peel
2 tablespoons lemon juice
3 pints strawberries
  Sugar substitute (optional)

1. Preheat oven to 350°F. Coat 8×4-inch loaf pan with nonstick cooking spray; set aside. Combine flour, baking powder, baking soda and salt in large bowl.

2. Combine sour cream, milk, sugar, oil, egg substitute, lemon peel and lemon juice in medium bowl. Stir sour cream mixture into flour mixture until well blended; pour batter into prepared pan.

3. Bake 45 to 50 minutes or until toothpick inserted into center comes out clean. Cool cake in pan 20 minutes. Remove to wire rack; cool completely. Meanwhile, slice strawberries. Sprinkle to taste with sugar substitute, if desired. Slice cake and serve with strawberries.

Makes 16 servings

Nutrients per Serving (1 slice with about 3 tablespoons strawberries):
Calories: 180, **Calories from Fat:** 29%, **Total Fat:** 6g, **Saturated Fat:** 1g, **Cholesterol:** 4mg, **Sodium:** 264mg, **Carbohydrate:** 28g, **Dietary Fiber:** 2g, **Protein:** 4g

Dietary Exchanges: 1 Starch, 1 Fruit, 1 Fat

Sweet Potato Phyllo Wraps

¾ **cup mashed sweet potato**
¾ **teaspoon vanilla**
½ **teaspoon ground cinnamon**
 4 **sheets frozen phyllo dough, thawed**
   Butter-flavored cooking spray
 4 **tablespoons finely chopped pecans**
 1 **tablespoon light maple syrup**
   Fresh strawberries (optional)

1. Preheat oven to 375°F. Line baking sheet with parchment paper. Combine sweet potato, vanilla and cinnamon in small bowl; mix well.

2. Unroll phyllo dough, keeping sheets in a stack. Cover with large sheet of waxed paper and damp kitchen towel. Remove 1 sheet at a time; place on work surface with short side facing you. Spray edges lightly with cooking spray.

3. Spread 3 tablespoons sweet potato mixture across short edge of phyllo dough. Sprinkle with 1 tablespoon chopped pecans. Roll up. Cut into thirds; place on prepared baking sheet. Repeat with remaining phyllo sheets, sweet potato mixture and pecans.

4. Spray tops of wraps with cooking spray. Bake 15 to 20 minutes or until golden brown. Remove from oven; drizzle with maple syrup. Garnish with strawberries.

Makes 12 wraps

Nutrients per Serving (3 wraps with ¾ teaspoon maple syrup):
Calories: 165, **Calories from Fat:** 38%, **Total Fat:** 7g,
Saturated Fat: 1g, **Cholesterol:** 0mg, **Sodium:** 120mg,
Carbohydrate: 24g, **Dietary Fiber:** 3g, **Protein:** 3g

Dietary Exchanges: 1½ Starch, 1 Fat

Cranberry Apple Crisp

3 cups peeled and sliced apples
2 cups fresh cranberries
1 cup EQUAL® SPOONFUL*
½ cup EQUAL® SPOONFUL**
⅓ cup all-purpose flour
¼ cup chopped pecans
¼ cup stick butter or margarine, melted

May substitute 24 packets EQUAL® sweetener.

**May substitute 12 packets EQUAL® sweetener.*

• Combine apples, cranberries and 1 cup Equal® Spoonful in ungreased 10-inch pie pan.

• Combine ½ cup Equal® Spoonful, flour, pecans and butter in separate bowl. Sprinkle mixture over top of apples and cranberries.

• Bake in preheated 350°F oven about 1 hour or until bubbly and lightly browned. *Makes 8 servings*

Tip: This crisp is delicious served as an accompaniment to pork or poultry or with frozen yogurt as a dessert.

Nutrients per Serving (½ cup crisp):
Calories: 150, **Calories from Fat:** 50%, **Total Fat:** 9g,
Saturated Fat: 4g, **Cholesterol:** 16mg, **Sodium:** 62mg,
Carbohydrate: 18g, **Dietary Fiber:** 3g, **Protein:** 1g

Dietary Exchanges: 1 Fruit, 2 Fat

Fresh cranberries are readily available September through December. Since they are usually not available other months of the year, buy an extra bag or two for the freezer. Cranberries freeze well and can usually be added to recipes without thawing.

cold & creamy

Honeydew Melon Sorbet

⅔ **cup water**
⅔ **cup measure-for-measure sugar substitute**
4 **teaspoons lemon juice**
1 **honeydew melon**

1. Combine water, sugar substitute and lemon juice in small saucepan. Bring to a boil. Boil 1 minute. Cool 15 minutes to room temperature.

2. Remove rind and seeds from melon. Cut into pieces. Place melon in food processor or blender. Process until smooth. Add sugar substitute mixture. Process until blended.

3. Pour into 8-inch square metal pan. Freeze at least 4 hours or overnight. Let stand at room temperature 15 minutes to soften slightly before serving. Scoop into dessert dishes.

Makes 8 servings

Nutrients per Serving (½ cup):
Calories: 46, **Calories from Fat:** 3%, **Total Fat:** 0g,
Saturated Fat: 0g, **Cholesterol:** 0mg, **Sodium:** 23mg,
Carbohydrate: 14g, **Dietary Fiber:** 1g, **Protein:** <1g

Dietary Exchanges: 1 Fruit

Strawberry-Banana Granité

2 ripe medium bananas, peeled and sliced (about 2 cups)
2 cups unsweetened frozen strawberries *(do not thaw)*
¼ cup no-sugar-added strawberry pourable fruit*
Whole fresh strawberries (optional)
Fresh mint leaves (optional)

*3 tablespoons no-sugar-added strawberry fruit spread combined with 1 tablespoon warm water can be substituted.

1. Place banana slices in plastic bag; freeze until firm.

2. Place frozen banana slices and frozen strawberries in food processor container. Let stand 10 minutes for fruit to soften slightly. Add pourable fruit. Remove plug from top of food processor to allow air to be incorporated. Process until smooth, scraping down sides of container frequently. Serve immediately. Garnish with fresh strawberries and mint leaves, if desired. Freeze leftovers.   *Makes 5 servings*

Note: Granité can be transferred to airtight container and frozen up to 1 month. Let stand at room temperature 10 minutes to soften slightly before serving.

Nutrients per Serving (⅔ cup granité):
Calories: 87, **Calories from Fat:** 3%, **Total Fat:** <1g,
Saturated Fat: <1g, **Cholesterol:** 0mg, **Sodium:** 2mg,
Carbohydrate: 22g, **Dietary Fiber:** 2g, **Protein:** 1g

Dietary Exchanges: 1½ Fruit

Fruit Freezies

**1½ cups (12 ounces) canned or thawed frozen peach
    slices, drained**
¾ cup peach nectar
1 tablespoon sugar
¼ to ½ teaspoon coconut extract (optional)

1. Place peaches, nectar, sugar and coconut extract, if
desired, in food processor or blender container; process
until smooth.

2. Spoon 2 tablespoons fruit mixture into each section of ice
cube tray.*

3. Freeze until almost firm. Insert frill pick into center of each
cube; freeze until firm.   *Makes 12 servings*

*Or, pour ⅓ cup fruit mixture into each of 8 plastic molds or small
paper or plastic cups. Freeze until almost firm. Insert wooden stick
into center of each mold; freeze until firm.*

Apricot Freezies: Substitute canned apricot halves for
peach slices and apricot nectar for peach nectar.

Pear Freezies: Substitute canned pear slices for peach
slices, pear nectar for peach nectar and almond extract for
coconut extract, if desired.

Pineapple Freezies: Substitute crushed pineapple for peach
slices and unsweetened pineapple juice for peach nectar.

Mango Freezies: Substitute chopped fresh mango for peach
slices and mango nectar for peach nectar. Omit coconut
extract.

Nutrients per Serving (2 cubes):
Calories: 19, **Calories from Fat:** 1%, **Total Fat:** <1g,
Saturated Fat: <1g, **Cholesterol:** 0mg, **Sodium:** 2mg,
Carbohydrate: 5g, **Dietary Fiber:** <1g, **Protein:** <1g

Dietary Exchanges: ½ Fruit

Strawberry Granita

1 quart fresh strawberries, sliced
¼ cup powdered sugar
¼ cup water
2 tablespoons sugar substitute*
1 to 1½ tablespoons fresh lemon juice, divided

This recipe was tested with sucralose-based sugar substitute.

1. Combine strawberries, powdered sugar, water, sugar substitute and 1 tablespoon lemon juice in blender. Process until smooth. If necessary, add additional ½ tablespoon lemon juice.

2. Pour into 8-inch square baking pan. Cover with foil and freeze 2 hours or until slushy. Remove from freezer and stir to break mixture up into small chunks. Cover and return to freezer. Freeze 2 hours, then stir to break granita up again. Cover and freeze at least 4 hours or overnight.

3. To serve, scrape surface of granita with large metal spoon to shave off thin pieces. Spoon into individual bowls and serve immediately.   *Makes 8 servings*

Nutrients per Serving (¾ cup):
Calories: 54, **Calories from Fat:** 0%, **Total Fat:** 0g,
Saturated Fat: <1g, **Cholesterol:** 0mg, **Sodium:** 1mg,
Carbohydrate: 14g, **Dietary Fiber:** 1g, **Protein:** <1g

Dietary Exchanges: 1 Fruit

Cool Lime Cheesecake

1 cup graham cracker crumbs
3 tablespoons stick butter or margarine, melted
2 tablespoons EQUAL® SPOONFUL*
2 packages (8 ounces each) reduced-fat cream
    cheese, softened
⅔ cup EQUAL® SPOONFUL**
1 egg
2 egg whites
½ teaspoon grated lime peel
3 tablespoons fresh lime juice

*May substitute 3 packets EQUAL® sweetener.

**May substitute 16 packets EQUAL® sweetener.

• Combine graham cracker crumbs, butter and 2 tablespoons Equal® Spoonful in bottom of 8-inch springform pan or 8-inch cake pan; pat evenly onto bottom and ½ inch up side of pan. Bake in preheated 325°F oven 8 minutes.

• Beat cream cheese and ⅔ cup Equal® Spoonful in medium bowl until fluffy. Beat in egg, egg whites, lime peel and juice until well blended. Pour cream cheese mixture into prepared crust.

• Bake in 325°F oven 30 to 35 minutes or until center is almost set. Cool on wire rack. Refrigerate at least 3 hours before serving. *Makes 8 servings*

Nutrients per Serving:
Calories: 224, **Calories from Fat:** 58%, **Total Fat:** 15g, **Saturated Fat:** 8g, **Cholesterol:** 65mg, **Sodium:** 374mg, **Carbohydrate:** 15g, **Dietary Fiber:** 1g, **Protein:** 9g

Dietary Exchanges: 1 Starch, 1 Lean Meat, 2½ Fat

Creamy Strawberry-Orange Pops

1 container (6 ounces) strawberry sugar-free fat-free
   yogurt
¾ cup orange juice
2 teaspoons vanilla
2 cups frozen whole strawberries
1 packet sugar substitute *or* equivalent of
   2 teaspoons sugar
6 (7-ounce) paper cups
6 wooden sticks

1. Combine yogurt, orange juice and vanilla in food processor or blender. Cover and process until smooth.

2. Add strawberries and sugar substitute. Process until smooth. Pour into 6 paper cups, filling each about three-fourths full. Freezer 1 hour. Insert wooden stick into center of each. Freeze completely. Peel cup off each pop to serve.

Makes 6 servings

Nutrients per Serving (1 pop):
Calories: 97, **Calories from Fat:** 4%, **Total Fat:** <1g,
Saturated Fat: <1g, **Cholesterol:** 1mg, **Sodium:** 139mg,
Carbohydrate: 17g, **Dietary Fiber:** 1g, **Protein:** 6g

Dietary Exchanges: 1 Fruit, ½ Milk

tip

If you prefer frozen treats in a bowl, freeze the mixture in a shallow container and stir it once or twice while it is freezing. Then scrape the surface to shave off thin pieces and spoon them into a bowl.

Cold & Creamy Fruit Cups

1 package (8 ounces) fat-free cream cheese
1 cup fat-free sour cream
⅓ cup EQUAL® SPOONFUL*
2 to 3 teaspoons lemon juice
1 cup coarsely chopped fresh or canned peaches
1 cup fresh or frozen blueberries
1 cup fresh or unsweetened frozen raspberries or
    halved or quartered strawberries
1 cup cubed fresh or canned pineapple in juice
1 can (11 ounces) mandarin orange segments, drained
12 pecan halves, optional

*May substitute 8 packets EQUAL® sweetener.

• Beat cream cheese, sour cream, EQUAL® and lemon juice in medium bowl until smooth; gently mix in fruit.

• Spoon mixture into 12 paper-lined muffin cups, or spread in baking dish 10×6 inches. Garnish with pecan halves and additional fruit, if desired. Freeze until firm, 6 to 8 hours. Let stand at room temperature until slightly softened, 10 to 15 minutes, before serving.   *Makes 12 servings*

Tip: If made in a 10×6-inch baking dish; cut into squares and serve on lettuce-lined plates as a salad, or on plates with puréed strawberry or raspberry sauce for dessert.

Tip: The fruit mixture can be spooned into hollowed-out orange halves and frozen. Cut thin slices from bottom of orange halves so they will stand; place in muffin tins to freeze.

Nutrients per Serving (1 fruit cup):
Calories: 75, **Calories from Fat:** 0%, **Total Fat:** 0g,
Saturated Fat: 0g, **Cholesterol:** 3mg, **Sodium:** 130mg,
Carbohydrate: 14g, **Dietary Fiber:** 1g, **Protein:** 5g

Dietary Exchanges: 1 Fruit

Speedy Pineapple-Lime Sorbet

1 ripe pineapple, cut into cubes (about 4 cups)
⅓ cup frozen limeade concentrate
1 teaspoon grated lime peel
1 to 2 tablespoons fresh lime juice

1. Arrange pineapple in single layer on large baking sheet; freeze at least 1 hour or until very firm.*

2. Combine frozen pineapple, limeade, lime peel and lime juice in food processor; cover and process until smooth and fluffy. If mixture doesn't become smooth and fluffy, let stand 30 minutes to soften slightly; repeat processing. Serve immediately.   *Makes 8 servings*

Pineapple can be frozen up to 1 month in resealable freezer food storage bags.

Note: This dessert is best if served immediately, but it can be made ahead, stored in the freezer and then softened several minutes before being served.

Nutrients per Serving (½ cup sorbet):
Calories: 56, **Calories from Fat:** 5%, **Total Fat:** <1g,
Saturated Fat: <1g, **Cholesterol:** 0mg, **Sodium:** 1mg,
Carbohydrate: 15g, **Dietary Fiber:** 1g, **Protein:** <1g

Dietary Exchanges: 1 Fruit

tip

Keep a supply of frozen fruit on hand and you can easily turn it into a quick frozen dessert or smoothie with the addition of some flavorings, yogurt or milk.

Individual No-Bake Cheesecake Fruit Cups

1 cup quartered strawberries
1 cup diced peaches
3 tablespoons sugar substitute,* divided
¼ teaspoon ground ginger
5 ounces reduced-fat cream cheese, softened
3 tablespoons fat-free sour cream
2 tablespoons fat-free (skim) milk
1 teaspoon vanilla
¼ cup graham cracker crumbs**

*This recipe was tested with sucralose-based sugar substitute.

**Or, crush 2½ whole graham crackers.

1. Combine strawberries, peaches, 1 tablespoon sugar substitute and ginger in medium bowl. Toss gently to blend. Set aside.

2. Beat cream cheese, sour cream, milk, vanilla and remaining 2 tablespoons sugar substitute in medium bowl with electric mixer at medium speed until smooth.

3. Place about 3 tablespoons cream cheese mixture in each of four (4-ounce) custard cups. Sprinkle 1 tablespoon cracker crumbs evenly into each cup. Top with ½ cup berry mixture. Cover and refrigerate at least 1 hour.

Makes 4 servings

Nutrients per Serving (1 cheesecake cup):
Calories: 115, **Calories from Fat:** 30%, **Total Fat:** 4g,
Saturated Fat: 2g, **Cholesterol:** 12mg, **Sodium:** 162mg,
Carbohydrate: 17g, **Dietary Fiber:** 2g, **Protein:** 4g

Dietary Exchanges: ½ Starch, ½ Fruit, 1 Fat

cookies & cakes

Peanut Butter & Banana Cookies

¼ cup (½ stick) butter
½ cup mashed ripe banana
½ cup no-sugar-added natural peanut butter
¼ cup thawed frozen unsweetened apple juice
    concentrate
1 egg
1 teaspoon vanilla
1 cup all-purpose flour
½ teaspoon baking soda
¼ teaspoon salt
½ cup chopped salted peanuts
    Whole salted peanuts (optional)

1. Preheat oven to 375°F. Grease 2 cookie sheets.

2. Beat butter in large bowl until creamy. Add banana and peanut butter; beat until smooth. Blend in apple juice concentrate, egg and vanilla. Beat in flour, baking soda and salt. Stir in chopped peanuts.

3. Drop rounded tablespoonfuls of dough 2 inches apart onto prepared cookie sheets; top each with one whole peanut, if desired. Bake 8 minutes or until set. Cool completely on wire racks. Store in tightly covered container.

Makes 2 dozen cookies

Nutrients per Serving (1 cookie):
Calories: 100, **Calories from Fat:** 53%, **Total Fat:** 6g,
Saturated Fat: 2g, **Cholesterol:** 14mg, **Sodium:** 88mg,
Carbohydrate: 9g, **Dietary Fiber:** 1g, **Protein:** 3g

Dietary Exchanges: ½ Starch, 1½ Fat

Donut Spice Cakes

1 package (9 ounces) yellow cake mix
½ cup cold water
2 eggs
½ teaspoon ground cinnamon
¼ teaspoon ground nutmeg
2 teaspoons powdered sugar

1. Preheat oven to 350°F. Grease and flour 10 mini (½-cup) bundt pans.

2. Combine cake mix, water, eggs, cinnamon and nutmeg in medium bowl. Beat with electric mixer at high speed 4 minutes or until well blended.

3. Spoon about ¼ cup batter into each prepared bundt pan. Bake 13 minutes or until toothpick inserted near centers comes out clean and cakes spring back when lightly touched.

4. Cool in pans on wire racks 5 minutes. Remove cakes from pans. Serve warm or at room temperature. Sprinkle with powdered sugar just before serving.   *Makes 10 servings*

Prep Time: 10 minutes
Bake Time: 13 minutes

Nutrients per Serving (1 cake):
Calories: 127, **Calories from Fat:** 28%, **Total Fat:** 4g,
Saturated Fat: 1g, **Cholesterol:** 43mg, **Sodium:** 182mg,
Carbohydrate: 21g, **Dietary Fiber:** <1g, **Protein:** 2g

Dietary Exchanges: 1½ Starch, ½ Fat

Pink Peppermint Meringues

3 egg whites
⅛ teaspoon peppermint extract
5 drops red food coloring
½ cup superfine sugar*
6 sugar-free peppermint candies, finely crushed

*Or use ½ cup granulated sugar processed in food processor 1 minute until very fine.

1. Preheat oven to 200°F. Line 2 cookie sheets with parchment paper.

2. Beat egg whites in medium bowl with electric mixer at medium-high speed about 45 seconds or until frothy. Beat in extract and food coloring. Add sugar, 1 tablespoon at a time, while mixer is running. Beat until egg whites are stiff and glossy.

3. Drop meringue by teaspoonfuls into 1-inch mounds on prepared cookie sheets; sprinkle evenly with crushed candies.

4. Bake 2 hours or until meringues are dry when tapped. Transfer parchment paper with meringues to wire racks to cool completely.   *Makes about 74 meringues*

Nutrients per Serving (1 meringue):
Calories: 6, **Calories from Fat:** <1%, **Total Fat:** <1g,
Saturated Fat: 0g, **Cholesterol:** 0mg, **Sodium:** 3mg,
Carbohydrate: 2g, **Dietary Fiber:** 0g, **Protein:** <1g

Dietary Exchanges: Free

Banana Poppy Seed Cake

1 box (about 18 ounces) white cake mix
1 cup water
4 egg whites
2/3 cup unsweetened applesauce
1 package (4-serving size) banana cream fat-free
    sugar-free instant pudding and pie filling mix
1/4 cup poppy seeds

1. Preheat oven to 350°F. Coat 11×17-inch jelly-roll pan with nonstick cooking spray.

2. Mix cake mix, water, egg whites, applesauce, pudding mix and poppy seeds together until well blended. Spread in prepared pan.

3. Bake 18 minutes or until toothpick inserted into center comes out clean. Serve warm or let cool before serving.

Makes 24 servings

Nutrients per Serving (1 piece):
Calories: 108, **Calories from Fat:** 25%, **Total Fat:** 3g,
Saturated Fat: <1g, **Cholesterol:** 0mg, **Sodium:** 198mg,
Carbohydrate: 19g, **Dietary Fiber:** <1g, **Protein:** 2g

Dietary Exchanges: 1 Starch, ½ Fat

tip

A jelly-roll pan is a rectangular baking pan with sides that are one inch high. Traditionally it is used to prepare a sponge cake, which is then spread with a filling (usually jam or jelly) and rolled up. Jelly-roll pans can also used to make thin sheet cakes.

Soft Ginger Cookies

2 cups all-purpose flour
1½ teaspoons ground ginger
1 teaspoon baking soda
¼ teaspoon salt
¼ teaspoon ground cinnamon
¼ teaspoon ground cloves
¼ cup packed light brown sugar
¼ cup canola oil
¼ cup molasses
½ cup fat-free sour cream
1 egg white

1. Preheat oven to 350°F.

2. Combine flour, ginger, baking soda, salt, cinnamon and cloves in large bowl. Beat brown sugar, oil and molasses in large bowl with electric mixer at medium speed 1 minute or until smooth. Add sour cream and egg white; beat until well blended. Gradually add flour mixture to wet ingredients, beating on low speed until well blended.

3. Drop dough by rounded tablespoonfuls 2 inches apart onto ungreased cookie sheets. Flatten dough to ⅛-inch thickness with bottom of glass lightly sprayed with nonstick cooking spray.

4. Bake 10 minutes or until tops of cookies puff up and spring back when lightly touched. Cool 2 minutes on cookie sheets. Remove to wire racks; cool completely.

Makes about 2½ dozen cookies

Nutrients per Serving (1 cookie):
Calories: 60, **Calories from Fat:** 30%, **Total Fat:** 2g,
Saturated Fat: <1g, **Cholesterol:** <1mg, **Sodium:** 65mg,
Carbohydrate: 10g, **Dietary Fiber:** <1g, **Protein:** 1g

Dietary Exchanges: ½ Starch, ½ Fat

Cocoa Nutty Bites

1 cup creamy unsweetened natural peanut butter
½ cup light brown sugar, not packed
¼ cup sucralose-based sugar substitute
1 tablespoon unsweetened cocoa powder
½ teaspoon ground cinnamon
¼ teaspoon salt
¼ teaspoon ground ginger
1 egg, beaten

1. Preheat oven to 350°F. Combine peanut butter, brown sugar, sugar substitute, cocoa, cinnamon, salt and ginger in medium bowl. Add egg; stir until well blended.

2. Shape dough into 24 (1-inch) balls. Place on ungreased cookie sheets. Flatten balls with fork to ½-inch thickness.

3. Bake 10 to 12 minutes or until cookies are firm and lightly browned. Cool on cookie sheets 5 minutes. Remove to wire racks; cool completely.   *Makes 24 cookies*

Note: This simple recipe is unusual because it doesn't contain any flour—but it still makes great cookies!

Nutrients per Serving (1 cookie):
Calories: 85, **Calories from Fat:** 55%, **Total Fat:** 5g,
Saturated Fat: 1g, **Cholesterol:** 9mg, **Sodium:** 79mg,
Carbohydrate: 8g, **Dietary Fiber:** 1g, **Protein:** 3g

Dietary Exchanges: ½ Starch, 1 Fat

Pumpkin Cake

3 cups all-purpose flour
2 teaspoons ground cinnamon
1 teaspoon baking soda
1 teaspoon ground nutmeg
1 teaspoon ground cloves
½ teaspoon baking powder
½ teaspoon salt
1 cup sucralose-sugar blend
½ cup canola oil
½ cup unsweetened applesauce
1 can (15 ounces) solid-pack pumpkin
¾ cup cholesterol-free egg substitute

1. Preheat oven to 325°F. Spray 13×9-inch baking pan with nonstick cooking spray; set aside. Combine flour, cinnamon, baking soda, nutmeg, cloves, baking powder and salt in medium bowl.

2. Beat sucralose-sugar blend, oil and applesauce in large bowl with electric mixer at medium speed 1 minute or until smooth. Beat in pumpkin and egg substitute until well blended.

3. Gradually add flour mixture to pumpkin mixture, beating until just blended. Do not overmix.

4. Pour batter into prepared pan. Bake 1 hour, 20 minutes or until toothpick inserted into center comes out clean. Cool completely in pan on wire rack. Cut into 24 pieces.

Makes 24 servings

Nutrients per Serving:
Calories: 150, **Calories from Fat:** 30%, **Total Fat:** 5g,
Saturated Fat: <1g, **Cholesterol:** 0mg, **Sodium:** 127mg,
Carbohydrate: 22g, **Dietary Fiber:** 1g, **Protein:** 3g

Dietary Exchanges: 1½ Starch, 1 Fat

Caribbean Cake Squares

1 package (9 ounces) yellow cake mix
2 egg whites
½ cup orange juice
2 cans (8 ounces each) crushed pineapple in juice
   Additional orange juice
1 tablespoon cornstarch
½ cup slivered almonds
½ cup flaked coconut
2 large ripe bananas
1 can (15 ounces) mandarin oranges, drained

1. Preheat oven to 350°F. Spray 13×9-inch baking pan with nonstick cooking spray.

2. Beat cake mix, egg whites and orange juice in medium bowl with electric mixer at medium speed 2 minutes or until well blended. Spoon batter evenly into prepared pan.

3. Bake 11 to 12 minutes or until toothpick inserted into center comes out clean. Cool in pan on wire rack.

4. Drain pineapple into 2 cup measure; add additional orange juice to measure 1½ cups liquid. Pour juice mixture into medium saucepan. Stir in cornstarch until smooth. Bring juice mixture to a boil over high heat, stirring constantly. Boil 1 minute, stirring constantly. Remove from heat.

5. Place almonds and coconut in large skillet; cook and stir over medium heat until light brown.

6. Spread pineapple over cake. Slice bananas and arrange over pineapple. Top with mandarin oranges. Carefully drizzle juice mixture evenly over topping. Sprinkle with almond mixture. Cover and refrigerate 1 to 4 hours.

Makes 16 servings

Nutrients per Serving (1 piece):
Calories: 148, **Calories from Fat:** 29%, **Total Fat:** 5g,
Saturated Fat: 1g, **Cholesterol:** <1mg, **Sodium:** 115mg,
Carbohydrate: 25g, **Dietary Fiber:** 2g, **Protein:** 2g

Dietary Exchanges: 1½ Starch, 1 Fat

Enlightened Banana Upside-Down Cake

½ cup sugar
1 tablespoon water
2 tablespoons butter
2 small bananas, sliced ¼ inch thick
1½ cups all-purpose flour
2 teaspoons baking powder
½ teaspoon salt
¾ cup sugar substitute*
¼ cup canola oil
¼ cup unsweetened applesauce
1 whole egg
2 egg whites
½ cup low-fat buttermilk
1 teaspoon vanilla

This recipe was tested with sucralose-based sugar substitute.

1. Preheat oven to 325°F. Heat sugar and water in small saucepan over medium-high heat until mixture is amber in color. Stir in butter. Pour mixture into 8-inch square nonstick baking pan. Arrange banana slices in sugar mixture.

2. Sift flour, baking powder and salt in medium bowl. Beat sugar substitute, oil and applesauce in large bowl with electric mixer at medium speed 1 minute. Beat in whole egg and egg whites one at a time. Add buttermilk and vanilla. Gradually add flour mixture, beating until blended.

3. Pour batter over bananas in pan. Bake 30 to 35 minutes or until toothpick inserted into center comes out clean. Cool 5 minutes in pan on wire rack; invert onto serving plate.

Makes 12 servings

Nutrients per Serving:
Calories: 184, **Calories from Fat:** 35%, **Total Fat:** 7g,
Saturated Fat: 2g, **Cholesterol:** 23mg, **Sodium:** 191mg,
Carbohydrate: 27g, **Dietary Fiber:** 1g, **Protein:** 3g

Dietary Exchanges: 1½ Starch, ½ Fruit, 1 Fat

Oatmeal-Date Cookies

½ cup packed light brown sugar
¼ cup margarine, softened
1 whole egg
1 egg white
1 tablespoon thawed frozen apple juice concentrate
1 teaspoon vanilla
1½ cups all-purpose flour
2 teaspoons baking soda
¼ teaspoon salt
1½ cups uncooked quick oats
½ cup chopped dates or raisins

1. Preheat oven to 350°F. Lightly coat cookie sheet with nonstick cooking spray; set aside.

2. Combine brown sugar and margarine in large bowl; mix well. Add egg, egg white, apple juice concentrate and vanilla; mix well.

3. Add flour, baking soda and salt; mix well. Stir in oats and dates. Drop dough by teaspoonfuls onto prepared cookie sheet.

4. Bake 8 to 10 minutes or until edges are very lightly browned. (Centers should still be soft.) Cool 1 minute on cookie sheet. Remove to wire rack; cool completely.

Makes 3 dozen cookies

Nutrients per Serving (1 cookie):
Calories: 65, **Calories from Fat:** 27%, **Total Fat:** 2g,
Saturated Fat: <1g, **Cholesterol:** 6mg, **Sodium:** 106mg,
Carbohydrate: 11g, **Dietary Fiber:** 1g, **Protein:** 1g

Dietary Exchanges: 1 Starch

The publisher would like to thank the companies and organizations listed below for the use of their recipes and photographs in this publication.

Dole Food Company, Inc.

Equal® sweetener

The Hershey Company

Peanut Advisory Board